Climbing Lakeland Peaks

Other Dalesman books of related interest:

EXPLORING THE LAKELAND FELLS
MAP READING
PATHFINDER (Navigation and safety in the Hills)

Climbing Lakeland Peaks

202 fell tops over 2,000 feet

by
J.K. Fryer

Dalesman Books
1984

The Dalesman Publishing Company Ltd.,
Clapham, via Lancaster, LA2 8EB

First published 1984

ISBN: 0 85206 767 4

Phototypeset, printed and bound by Galava Printing Company Ltd, Nelson, Lancs.

Contents

Introduction 7

Some notes on the scheme 8

Beginnings 10

The Challenge and Organising 12

Day 1 - From the outskirts of Bassenthwaite village 14

Day 2 - From Carrock Mine, near Mungrisedale 16

Day 3 - From White Horse Inn, Threlkeld 18

Day 4 - From Lanthwaite Green, near Crummock Water 20

Day 5 - From Braithwaite 22

Day 6 - From Newlands Church 24

Day 7 - From Bowness Point, Ennerdale 26

Day 8 - From Bowness Point, Ennerdale 28

Day 9 - From Bowderdale, near Wasdale Head 30

Day 10 - From Wasdale Head 41

Day 11 - From Seathwaite 44

Day 12 - From Seathwaite 46

Day 13 - From Dungeon Ghyll, Langdale 48

Day 14 - From Dungeon Ghyll, Langdale 51

Day 15 - From Brotherilkeld, near Hard Knott Pass 53

Day 16 - From Wrynose Pass 54

Day 17 - From Dunmail Raise 56

Day 18 - From Dunmail Raise 58

Day 19 - From St. Johns in the Vale 60

Day 20 - From Glenridding 62

Day 21 - From Patterdale................................. 64

Day 22 - From North end of Kirkstone Pass................. 66

Day 23 - From Hartsop village 68

Day 24 - From Hartsop village 70

Day 25 - From Mardale (head of Haweswater) 72

Day 26 - From Mardale (head of Haweswater) 74

The Finish and the Future 76

The Peaks 77

Cover photographs:- Front: Great Gable from Esk Hause (Tom Parker). Back: Pike O' Stickle and Gimmer Crag from Rossett Crag (Tom Parker).

Introduction

IN latter years it has become increasingly obvious that modern society's notion of work is undergoing a fundamental change with far greater emphasis being placed upon effective use of leisure time. I was prompted to carry out this exercise for two reasons, first it reflects my own change from participation in organised sport to a serious considered approach to fell walking and secondly, because I hope to offer others a reasonably organised challenge based on my thoughts and recent experiences.

To begin with I will recall briefly my background in relation to the fells of Lakeland and how my interest was stimulated. Before moving on, I will discuss how the challenge developed and why I feel it is important, for there is little doubt many people conjure up notions on 'doing the tops' within a considered approach.

Following a discussion on the idea of 'doing the tops', a friend kindly handed me an excellent list of six figure reference points that totalled up to give 203 separate locations at 2,000 feet or above. The cartographic criteria may be considered relevant by the pedantic, but I support the comment made by a famous Lakeland author, A.M. Griffin, who concurred at the very least that anyone completing this list will have walked a considerable part of the high ground in Lakeland. Perhaps the only serious criticism of a 2,000 foot minimum is that much of the beauty is below this contour, such as Melbreak, Helm Crag and Angletarn Crag to name just three; however the list is limited which helps my challenge.

I will call the challenge 'All but One'. This is because among the 203 reference points you can read 172124 at 2,500 feet—this is in fact the summit of Pillar Rock. It should be emphasised clearly that this location is not for the average walker, it is for the rock climber only—although it can be viewed with safety from nearby.

Since I had already reached approximately one-third of the references before obtaining the reference points, my initial approach was necessarily different to the final challenge I present, and in fact on some occasions I have walked good distances to actually take in one location previously not considered.

No doubt there are many who regard the hills of Lakeland as sacred and will not welcome my scheme; to them I say 'you are entitled to your opinion'. I consider it good sense to try generating interest in a healthy leisure activity, for the two things about fell-walking are it takes time and effort to get virtually anywhere. When using up this time and effort the boredom and burdens of our modern world can be shelved or weathered as the case may be.

This then is my scheme 26 days out from 20 starting points and the possibility of 202 tops—'All but One' of the list.

J.K. Fryer

Some notes on the scheme

1. This is not a guide book, at the best it indicates a route. Others, in particular the superb Wainwright guides, are much better for this purpose.

2. The Ordnance Survey map is a must since all the reference points are closely related.

3. Planning is essential for any walk, the weather must always be considered, as must experience. The fells of Lakeland can be and frequently are dangerous places.

4. Take note of energy requirements and make sure that extra food and clothing are regular occupants of your haversack.

5. Be prepared to abandon or curtail any walk if it seems at all likely that a problem exists.

6. There will be suggested variations to my scheme; this is inevitable, but on the whole I consider it is practical in all aspects.

7. The starting points are concentrated in as few locations as I considered reasonable; this benefits camping, hosteling and other accommodation.

8. All these days out are something of a circular tour, since otherwise some of the longer ridges would certainly necessitate two cars: such as Red Screes (Kirkstone) to Clough Head (Threlkeld).

9. To attain the precise map location can often be something of a nonsense. I have generally in places such as Great Lingy Hill (Skiddaw) walked to somewhere near, but fortunately most places are obvious.

10. The writer assumes a general interest and knowledge of the area.

11. It should be noted that parking in the Lake district can be an awkward business and by no means all the starting points are

available all of the time, but generally speaking the planners are reasonable.

12. Alterations to footpaths are not unusual in the area. Whilst every effort is made here to avoid problems concerning rights of way there will always be some doubt. It is therefore of some importance that the would-be hillwalker keeps this in mind. Remember walls and fences are there for a purpose, costing time and money to erect in rough terrain.

13. Fell names are related to this list of tops; there are variations on maps.

14. The distances and heights are not precise, merely a general indication (see also note 6).

15. Ridges are occasionally referred to as a direction of walking.

16. For me the fells are a pleasure and I hope that some humour is evident in what follows.

Beginnings

I HAVE lived the greater part of my life within a few miles of the Lake District National Park which probably makes me more of a 'local' than many who derive pleasure from the area.

My interest in the fells was not stimulated by any particular event or set of circumstances as far as I can remember, but I do recall my first visit to Loweswater. In the early 1950s when motor cars were a relative novelty, and mercifully television much the same, I received a bicycle as a Christmas present and in the spring of that year I went, together with my father, on a cycle ride that took us to Loweswater village. We ate spring-onion sandwiches and drank fresh water from a stream near the roadside, just before the road almost touches the lakeside. The day was something different and for me the peace and quietness was unusual. At that time the steel industry in West Cumberland was much more active than at present and the air was continuously filled with the associated sounds.

When my family moved into the area they left many roots in the West Riding of Yorkshire, and on the usually annual visit down there we travelled on the West Yorkshire bus service from Keswick to Bradford. The journey at that time was much longer and the ascent of Dunmail Raise, even in a bus, was something to remember, by no means least for the distinctive outline of Helm Crag, better known to me as the 'Lion and the Lamb' because of the rock formation near its summit.

I was 17 when with other apprentices I spent a Bank Holiday walking over Skiddaw; it was a sweltering hot day and the hill was crowded with people. Even in the haze of such a hot summer day, Derwentwater was like a sparkling crystal patch way down below— this impressed me more than anything else. The top of a large hill was not what I had expected, perhaps I was taken in by the weather that day, and certainly I have experienced my share of inferior conditions since then. The small tarn that nestles between Skiddaw and Carl Side received eight weary feet relieved of their commando-soled steel toe-capped United Steel Company's boots; no doubt the water promptly heated up as we bathed blistered feet.

Later I was to take any opportunity that came my way for a

fell walk or ramble, but these were less frequent since money and transport were not two of my strong points.

At the age of 22 I recall being in an office and talking with a quiet, serious Yorkshireman who was about 10 years my senior. We chatted about our leisure. After filling his ears with the vanity that can only be uttered by a rugby player, I eventually heard him say he was going to climb Scafell Pike that coming Sunday. I played my rugby on the Saturday and we duly climbed Scafell Pike on the Sunday, although I cannot recall the way we ascended—I got my first taste of nerves when descending by the path that accompanies Piers Gill downwards to Wasdale. The combination of wearly limbs and sights of that fearful drop into Piers Gill 'rooted' me for a little while. Although I have passed this way many times since, this huge ravine always makes me cringe. Thus I learned my respect for the hills without any injury—even here the mind can cause problems sufficient to deter foolishness. Then my life changed again following my marriage; night school and rugby were then a high priority for a few years and I was restricted. There followed an association with a father and two sons with many long walks, and being able to drive opened up new opportunities for a period of time. This association tapered off when they took to rock climbing, but nevertheless, I was on my way to real satisfaction. After concluding my rugby playing, I followed this with several trips to the Scottish Highlands and frequent visits into the Lake District National Park.

I began to look for something new, a different route, different weather, even nights out on the fells, until eventually I was given this list of compass bearings above the 2,000 foot mark. Although this list was broken down into areas, it was not in this form that my scheme to reach all these points was devised. Prior to obtaining this information many of the fells had already been climbed by me and, naturally, to complete the tops I adopted a personalised method as I mentioned in the introduction. When I reached the final point of my journey I can remember the feeling of having achieved something and now I look upon my days out with a difference, trying wherever possible to add variety to the network of walks already completed.

The Challenge and Organising

AFTER superimposing my various thoughts on to a fresh copy of the one-inch Ordnance Survey map, eventually a realistic method of tackling the 2,000 footers became apparent. To think in these terms I tried to consider those less fortunate who do not reside so near to the National Park, when a visit is as much based on the economics as the desire to seek the high ground—and in all probability this would be the majority.

Dependent from which direction the would-be challenger comes into the National Park, dictates the ease of access to a particular starting point which in turn will decide on the necessity to find a camp site, hostel or one of the great variety of hotels, farmhouses, guest houses and rented properties that are available. Certainly there is no shortage of choice in most cases, but with some of the longer walks it is perhaps desirable to be in a position to forego the domestic aspects of such trips.

It is of vital importance to treat all of these days in the scheme with respect; even though some are much easier than others, factors outside the layout of an area will always have a major effect. Weather conditions frequently change and I have generally found the telephone forecast from Windermere to be a good indication; this particular forecast is supported by the ranger service who report on underfoot conditions at high level. Sitting in my lounge a few miles from the area is no guarantee of knowing the prospects and for those a greater distance away, the change can be even more dramatic. Although poor conditions can be a deterrent, it is by no means final, but personally my strongest desire is to know where I am and, what's more, to be in a position to see the view around me. Misty conditions can have their own interest, but for example Skiddaw when the visibility is poor seems much less attractive than it can be, and actually certain reference points would be rather difficult to pinpoint in thick cloud on some fells.

Each person will find his or her own ideas on fell-walking inter-mingled with the general guidelines talked about by those in authority on the subject. However, there are certain specific requirements that must be adhered to. I refer of course to ample clothing, plenty of food, survival gear, whistle, torch, map and compass. Before undertaking some of the longer days it would be essential to study the area, making notes concerning routes off the high ground—'Naismith's rule' is one thing, changeable conditions another. Also it is well to realise your limitations and to build up to the longer days—running up the underground escalator is no substitute for a strong head wind at the end of a long day in the fells. Planning is vital; to many this will be second nature, to others it will need some thought.

To rush the challenge is to spoil much of what can be achieved but to combine this with a long drawn out holiday programme will be rewarding—a different way of life, with a tangible objective for most people, for unlike the 'Munro' tops, this is a far more realistic proposition.

Perhaps a word of warning: many of these walks are not designed to 'get the idea' of fell-walking, they are for those already involved. Therefore I make the necessary assumption that some honest endeavour and interest has been pursued.

Time is of great importance. An early start or a late one is dependent on the situation and it is important to gauge the heights and distance. Equally the nature of the terrain will dictate the duration of a day—Great Lingy Hill in very wet conditions can, for example, be a tiresome and time-consuming business. At all times it must be accepted that the conditions should dictate proceedings and plans are to be made accordingly.

There are of course many organisations involved in the National Park, but personally I always feel the peace and quiet of greater benefit and would much rather be in a party of three at the outside, whilst admitting that I do most of my walking alone. For me the attraction of being alone is that you only need consider yourself, your pace, your equipment and so on, whereas the complications of groups can cause more time being spent getting to the hill than actually climbing it. However, this is a selfish notion and the economics for many will dictate the means of attacking this challenge.

So then, the main guideline is a safety consciousness. Always leave word on your route and expected time of return, making sure that as far as possible the specific needs noted earlier are catered for and that conditions are, wherever possible, anticipated and do not come as a shock. There is no substitute for research and providing fitness and equipment are good this is a challenge of great value.

Day 1

Tops 1 - 7 inclusive

Start and finish at Bassenthwaite village.

1. Great Calva
2. Sale How
3. Lonscale Fell
4. Skiddaw—Lowman

5. Skiddaw
6. Carl Side
7. Longside

Schematic/Cartographic Route

(**Warning:** Always consult Ordnance Survey Map, ensure good use of compass).

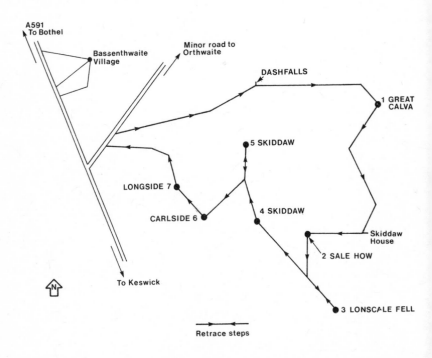

Retrace steps

1. Start and finish point 236310 (nr. Bassenthwaite Village). The route to Great Calva can be varied, but perhaps the least demanding would be a short road section then the bridleway to Dash

14

Falls. Once at the head of Dash Falls the fence can be followed heading approx. N.E. then E. passing over Little Calva and continuing on to **Great Calva 2,265ft (291312 Ref.)**.

2. From this splendid vantage point it's straight down through the grouse land heading for Skiddaw House. This can be done by descending the shortest route to the house's supply path, i.e., 283303 approx, or heading for the footbridge at 291296. When a glance round the somewhat imposing situation of Skiddaw House is complete, it is a straightforward slog up to **Sale How 2,200ft (277286 Ref.)**

3. To achieve our next objective, Lonscale Fell, there seems to be no obvious rapid solution; the choice is therefore to (a) Descend to Sale How Beck and pick up the Burnt Horse path which follows on towards the top, or (b) Take the shortest route to join the main path from Underscar then descend by crossing Jenkin Hill to the top, or perhaps (c) Skirt round Jenkin Hill holding height until joining up with the gate and wall thus having detoured from the Underscar to Skiddaw Path. **Lonscale Fell 2,344ft (286271 Ref.)**.

4. Simply back to the fence/wall and cross the main Skiddaw path, it is a straightforward and obvious detour up to a small undulation before going 700ft up and reaching the prominent **Skiddaw Little Man 2,837ft (267278 Ref.)**

5. Down a little then up the last 400ft to attain **Skiddaw Summit 3.053ft (Ref. 261291)**. The summit is invariably busy with fine virtually uninterrupted views all round, a giant in its own right.

6. The next stage is to go back towards the South top, i.e. retrace steps. The path down to Carl Side is not too problematic, basically in a S. Westerly direction. The coll supports a tiny pool. The move to Carl Side is a few yards across undulating grassy slopes. **Carl Side 2,400ft (255281 Ref.)**. This is approximately 1 mile from Skiddaw summit.

7. Along the N.W. ridge towards Longside, and for me perhaps the most impressive part of the Skiddaw group, the path is easy going and a delight. **Longside 2,405ft (249284 Ref.)**.

Again continue N.W. and in a third of a mile with a short ascent one arrives at Ullock Pike 2,330ft but this is not segregated by my list. From this point a straightforward descent of 1,800ft brings us back to our starting point. (Try to follow the path and save damaging boundary walls and/or fences).

13/14 miles; approx. 4,000ft of ascent.

Day 2

Tops 8 - 15 inclusive

Start and finish at Mosedale, near Mungrisedale

8.	Carrock Fell	12 & 13.	Great Sca Fell
9.	High Pike	14.	The Knott
10 & 11.	Great Lingy Hill	15.	Coomb Height

Schematic/Cartographic Route

(**Warning:** Always consult Ordnance Survey Map, ensure good use of compass).

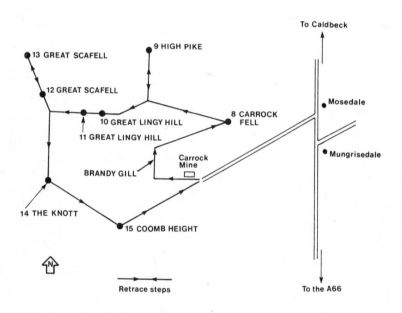

8. Start and finish at Carrock Mine (328328 Ref.). To attain Carrock summit can be done by going back down the road first to Mosedale and heading N.W., but for my money the most interesting route is up past the mine into Brandygill. At some opportune point near 322339 cut off leading due west for 1 mile to reach **Carrock Fell 2,174ft (342336)**, a historic and famous landmark with its tumuli.

9.   From Carrock Fell to our next high point, High Pike, is
             steady walking over pathless ground generally going west
but turning north and up the final drag on to the top of **High Pike**
2,157ft (319350 Ref.). A beautiful seat with inscription commemor-
ates a 'loved one'. This is perhaps more touching than most of
Lakeland's headstones—I feel saddened on every occasion I visit this
place.

10 & 11. Great Lingy Hill has two tops just above the 2,000ft mark,
             the first at **310339** approx. ¾ mile from High Pike, the
second at **303338** a further third of a mile or so—heavy going this
lot in bad weather. (A good dry spell or hard frost are needed here—
saves wet feet).

12 & 13. To reach Great Sca is a toil of a pleasure, reference my
             previous comments. What a 'boggy' area is Miller Moss—
why monstrous bogs get called moss is beyond me or rather I want it
to be so. Almost due west is the highest point of **Great Sca Fell**
at **2,100ft** and **292338** reference. A further short walk N.W. brings
up **Ref. 291342** at **2,050ft,** this being the second top. Now retrace
steps back over **292338** and move towards the next top.

14.   To reach **The Knott** it is a mere ¾ mile and 250ft of ascent
             and at **2,329ft** this is the highest point of the day
(Ref. 296330).

15.   The walk to **Coomb Height 2,058ft (Ref. 311327)** is the
             easiest part of the day; it is usually pleasantly airy strolling
down this broad ridge. From Coomb Height down is an interesting
but slow descent; history fills the air with the mine and the sight of
Carrock's distinctive top looming ahead. Indeed with the mine
operational it is a curious blend.

11/12 miles; approx. 2,500ft of ascent.

Day 3

Tops 16 - 21 inclusive

Start and finish at White Horse Inn, Threlkeld

16.	Blencathra	18 & 19.	Bannerdale Crags
17.	Knowe Crags	20 & 21.	Bowscale Fell

Schematic/Cartographic Route

(**Warning:** Always consult Ordnance Survey Map, ensure good use of compass).

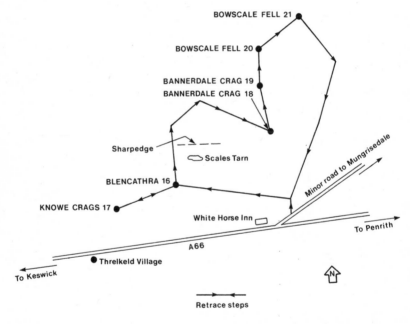

16. Start and finish at White Horse Inn, Threlkeld (342269).
Take (on foot) the little back road that edges Souther Fell turning up into Mousethwaite Comb at (347272). This path winds its way to the level ground between Souther Fell and Blencathra. The awe-inspiring sight of Sharp Edge comes into view; that way to the top is no ordinary route and those with nervous disorders or no experience should avoid it like the plague. Meanwhile over Scales Fell follow the crag line all the way to **Blencathra (Saddleback) Summit 2,847ft (323277 Ref.)**

18

17. Continue 'over' the summit heading along the crags and south-east to the rise of **Knowe Crags** which at **2,600ft** is our second top of the day **(Ref. 312270).**

18 & 19. It is possible to hold this height and follow a line to Foule Crag. However, it is far more interesting to retrace to the 323277 mark and then follow the path that allows a look down Sharp Edge and to Scales Tarn. Our route continues to 328292 before heading south-east over onto **Bannerdale's** two tops, first, i.e., **2,200ft (336290 Ref.),** and then back N.W. onto our second, **329296** for this point **(2,100ft).**

20 & 21. A natural, almost northerly walk reaches **Bowscale Fell's** highest point of **2,306ft (Ref. 333305).** Edging north the view down to Bowscale Tarn is impressive—the next top is easily attained at **340310—2,200ft.** From this point the choices of route back to the car are plentiful: (a) back over Bannerdale Crags and down at White Horse Bent before going south up and over into Mousethwaite again, or (b) drop off Bowscale into upper Mungrisedale following the River Glenderackin back to White Horse Bent, or (c) via the minor road round Souther Fell, or (d) for the real mad things, up over Souther Fell (which from my recollection was purgatory at the conclusion of a day).

10/11 miles; approx. 3,600ft of ascent.

Day 4

Tops 22 - 28 inclusive

Start and finish near Crummock Water

22 & 23. Whiteside   26. Grasmoor
      24. Hopegill Head   27. Wandhope
      25. Ladyside Pike   28. Whiteless Pike

Schematic/Cartographic Route

(**Warning:** Always consult Ordnance Survey Map, ensure good use
      of compass).

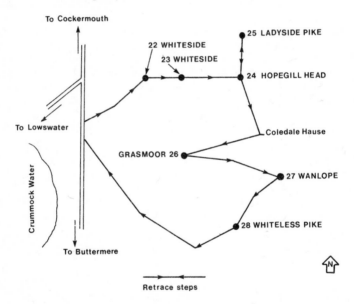

22 & 23. Start and finish at Lanthwaite Green (Ref. 160208). Across
         Lanthwaite Green, Gasgale Gill, up over Whin Ben direct
on to **Whiteside,** main top at **2,317ft (Ref. 171219).** Progress
easterly (in general) along this beautiful ridge across the east top at
2,250ft (Ref. 174222).

24.   The east top of Whiteside continues in a natural ridge until
         it reaches Hopegill Head—a magnificent point 'in the air' it
falls all ways (like Steeple and Catstycam). **Hopegill Head 2,525ft
(Ref. 186224).**

20

25. A slight detour at this point is essential to keep any projected tour within reasonable time limits. Descend north off Hopegill Head, very steep at first but quite safe. Keep crags to right—continue to **Ladyside Pike (185228), 2,300 + ft**, an interesting place and a rarely populated top, then retrace your steps back to Hopegill Head.

26. Heading south-east and then south over Sand Hill brings us to Coledale House. Take a S.W. flank towards Grasmoor top, keep the broken crags well to the right and take in the splendid views of Brackenthwaite Fell. Grasmoor is a big hill by any standards and if time allows have a look down Grasmoor End and pick out your car 2,000ft below (no bother if there's no mist). **Grasmoor Summit 2,791ft (Ref. 175203).**

27. From the summit follow the southern flank this time and drop down going generally east then south-east to **Wandhope (188197) at 2,533ft.)**

28. Regain the main 'back O'Grasmoor' path and head S.W. towards **Whiteless Pike 2,159ft (180190 Ref)**, a grand little hill. Reach Ref. 179176. From this point a choice exists: either walk back over Low Bank towards Hause Point on Crummock or go down the valley direct to Rannerdale. In any event there is little choice but some road work back up to Lanthwaite Green, although the lower flanks of Grasmoor can offer an interesting half hour or so.

10/11 miles; approx. 3,500ft of ascent.

Day 5

Tops 29 - 34 inclusive

Start and finish at Braithwaite

29 & 30.   Grisedale Pike
    31.   Eel Crag
    32.   Sail

33.   Scar Crags
34.   Causey Pike

Schematic/Cartographic Route

(**Warning:** Always consult Ordnance Survey Map, ensure good use
      of compass).

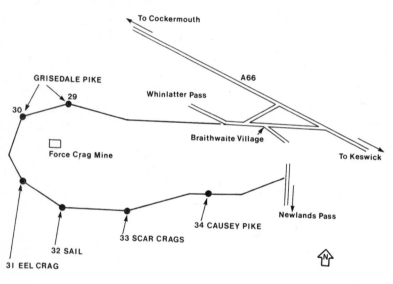

29 & 30. Start and finish in Braithwaite (222236). Up Kinnfell
heading south-west follow ridge all the way on to **Grisedale
Pike (199226) - 2,593 ft**, a top with four easy ways off. On the way to
Coledale Hause you pass over **193221—2,300ft**, the second top
of Grisedale Pike.

31.   At Coledale Hause take your pick but get up to the survey
column point on Eel Crags—what a view from here!
(No problems with the north shoulder on **Eel Crag**—steep at first
but O.K.). **193203—2,649ft**.

32.   Move off East and on to **Sail** (good ridge this). Summit
at **199203—2,500 ft** +, undulating walking but good view.
Turn slightly north towards Scar Crags; the route is never in any
doubt.

33.   **Scar Crags** is what its name implies, but quite narrow.
Good high level walking; the summit is at **208206—**
2,205ft.

34.   **Causey Pike**, the last part of this day, is something of a
surprise. It falls quite sharply nearly all around at **219209—**
2,000 ft. It is a spectacular end to the day's 'high tops'.

From here down is anyone's guess. In order to shorten the road
work it can be a good thing to head north-east and down over
Stile End or Barrow, but the choice is there once off the summit
crags. It is easy to descend straight over Causey Pike but the road
walk is left again, and apart from hurting boots in summer it takes
time dodging cars on the narrow road back to Braithwaite.

10/11 miles; approx. 4,000ft of ascent.

Day 6

Tops 35 - 40 inclusive

Start and finish at Newlands Valley

35.	Nitting Haws	38 & 39.	Hindscarth
36.	High Spy	40.	Robinson
37.	Dale Head		

Schematic/Cartographic Route

(**Warning:** Always consult Ordnance Survey Map, ensure good use of compass).

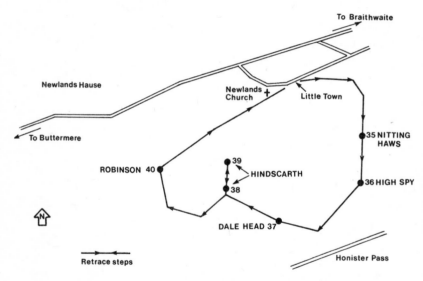

35. Start and finish at 235197, about ¼ mile from Newlands Church. The first objective is Maiden Moor. This can be attained by heading up over Knott End and High Crags or for the less adventurous go back to Little Town and take a right turn following the cart track then forking right to reach Hause Gate at 244192. From here head south over Black Crag, Maiden Moor to **Nitting Haws 2,050ft + (236170).**

36. The walk along to High Spy is easy at about ½ mile, but this high ground is blessed with superb views all round. No wonder it is a popular area for Sunday afternooners in summer. **High Spy top (234162) is 2,143ft.**

37.　　Heading in a southerly direction drop down to Rigg Head and Dalehead Tarn. From here one can head south-west and pick up the Honister to Dalehead path, but for me the direct but steep ascent dodging craggy outcrops is the better. **Dale Head 2,473ft (Ref. 223153)** is significantly the highest point of the day. Behold Newlands—commanding a magnificent prospect beneath and to all sides.

38 & 39. Move off from Dale Head following the N.W. ridge. The route is apparent—**Hindscarth**, first of two tops, is reached at **214160, 2,200ft**. The walk out on the huge spur that is Hindscarth brings one to a fine top at **216165, 2,385ft**. A grand place for a 'cuppa'.

40.　　A brief retracing of steps brings 212161 approx. This corner can be cut easily. The path then continues up on to **Robinson (202168) 2,417ft**.

The descent is a pleasure skirting south of Robinson crags and down on to High Snob Bank. Walk along the bracken path and at 1,100ft approx. drop into Little Dale and back to Newlands Church.

11/12 miles; approx. 3,500ft of ascent.

Day 7
Tops 41 - 48 inclusive
Start and finish at Ennerdale

41 & 42.	Great Borne	46.	Chapel Crags
43.	Starling Dodd	47.	High Stile
44.	Red Pike	48.	High Crag
45.	Dodd		

Schematic/Cartographic Route

(**Warning:** Always consult Ordnance Survey Map, ensure good use of compass).

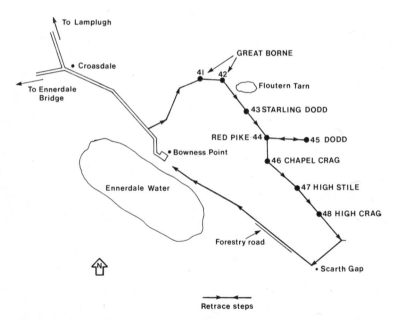

41 & 42. Start and finish at Bowness Point or a layby at 100166.

To tackle the day, as I see it, perhaps it is better to leave the car at Bowness Point and walk back to the above reference. At this place there is a sign pointing towards Floutern Tarn. At 120172 a fence will be the take off point (it being obvious so far) to go up Steel Brow, a tough 600ft but it gains a lot of height quickly. When the crag on the left is being displaced by sky then the first of **Great Borne's tops** is reached **(125165)** at **2,000ft**. From here to the highest point is a very short walk across a ravine to **124164** and the **2,019ft** main top. A more direct route is obvious heading N.E. from 110159 but this can be awkward in poor conditions.

43.   The path to our next objective is reasonably straightforward but the undulating lump called Starling Dodd is surprisingly hard to get up. I never know why since 450ft up off the dip between Great Borne and here seems a minor problem. However, **Starling Dodd** at **2,085ft** is at **142157**.

44.   The route from here to Red Pike is straightforward but it is best to pick up the cairn on Ling Comb edge (155163 approx.). From here up on to the summit of **Red Pike (160154)** **2,479ft** there is plenty to see.

45.   From Red Pike summit it is necessary to head·N.W. down the saddle that leads to Bleaberry Tarn and eventually Buttermere for at **165158** there is the important point called simply **Dodd** at **2,050ft** +

46 & 47. Back up on to Red Pike summit again then off round the top of **Chapel Crags**. At **164150** and **2,400ft** there is top No. 46 and then up on to **High Stile** top at **170148** and **2,644ft**, the highest point of our day. This is a superb top, the views over to Pillar and onwards to dear old Great Gable are among the best.

48.   Follow the narrower ridge to High Crag. On this section a glance in Burtness Comb can reward the eye and astonished looks greet those on the rock way below. At **180140** and **2,443ft, High Crag** is our final top of the day.

The choice is now obvious and perhaps the weather will dictate the decision. In poor conditions a run down Gamblin End to Scarth Gap is perhaps the quickest way off but then there is the prospect of a long trudge down the forestry path. If raining, the Youth Hostel at Black Sail can be host to the odd kindly soul, coffee and all that. However, a good day may make one happy to stay aloft, i.e., to walk back all the way or at least to Red Pike where a line of cairns heads one S.W. towards High Gillerthwaite and a couple of miles to Bowness Point (only).

12 to 15 miles. 3,000 to 3,500ft of ascent, approx., dependent on selection of route.

Day 8

Tops 49 - 53 inclusive

Start and finish at Ennerdale

49. Iron Crag
50. Caw Fell
51. Little Gowder Crag

52. Haycock
53. Seatallan

Schematic/Cartographic Route

(**Warning:** Always consult Ordnance Survey Map, ensure good use of compass).

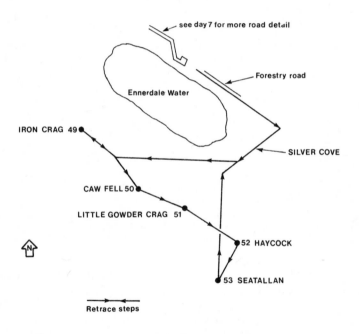

49. Start and finish at Bowness Point. Proceed along the northern shores of Ennerdale, crossing bridge at Gillerthwaite and into Silver Cove. A choice here but following the beck gains height quickly on to the ridge. At the wall 'T' junction turn right or N.W. on to **Iron Crag** top, **124119** and **2,100ft.**

50. Retrace steps past 'T' junction and up onto **Caw Fell** —old plane parts are to be found. Summit at **132110** and **2,288ft**, a lovely spot.

51 & 52. From here continue west to reach in one-third of a mile Little **Gowder Crag at 140110** and **2,350ft**. Some downhill work then up with the wall onto **Haycock** itself at **145107** and **2,618 ft**, the highest point of the day, significantly a giant.

53. From Haycock summit descend to the west of Gowder Crag at about 1,600ft. The final top of the day lies 650ft up in the form of **Seatallan**, a remote sort of hill of undulating proportions. The best line of approach is up its N.E. shoulder. Greendale Tarn and the distant Scafell with the might of Wasdale can be seen clearly. The summit is at **140084** and **2,266ft**.

Getting back to Bowness Point is now the problem besetting us. Perhaps the easiest is to pick up the Netherbeck (Wasdale) path to Haycock near Little Lad Crag; leave the path at the ridge descending into the beautiful Great Cove and go back down to join Silver Cove Beck—and unfortunately that dreary trudge up the lakeside. I am being somewhat unkind because a good early start can make this a pleasant day. The way back from Seatallan can be varied, of course, and this is reasonable in such a beautiful area and relatively unspoilt part of Lakeland, yet!

16/17 miles; approx. 4,500ft of ascent.

Day 9

Tops 54 - 65 inclusive

Start and finish at Wasdale

54.   Yewbarrow
55.   Stirrup Crag
56.   Red Pike (Wasdale)
57 - 59. Scoat Fell
60.   Steeple

61.   Black Crag
62.   Pillar
63.   Looking Stead
64 & 65. Kirk Fell

Schematic/Cartographic Route

(**Warning:**   Always consult Ordnance Survey Map, ensure good use of compass).

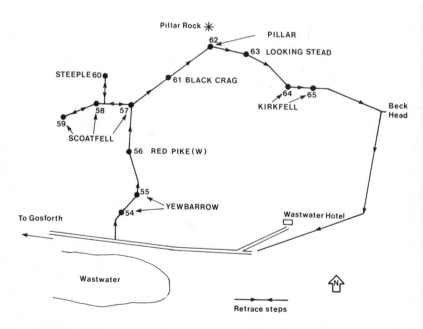

54 & 55. Start from 168068 (Bowderdale) Overbeck Bridge car park (alternatively leave car at Wasdale Head C.P. and do **road** at start). The great legend in his own lifetime, Joss Naylor, lives nearby. His performance in the fells will live forever, for whoever comes or goes it was the renowned Joss who named the sport of fell

30

running. As we walk from hill to hill it is well to recall that Joss has run the Ennerdale Horseshoe in 3½ hours which is quite something, and he is human!

However, we will begin our day by heading north and up on to **Yewbarrow**. From the left of the named Bell Rib the path goes over to the main top at **173085** and **2,058ft**. Continuing along the natural way a further rise brings Yewbarrow's second top named **Sturrup Crag** at **176093** and **2,009ft**. Along this top the Scafell group look majestic; on the eastern side to the N.E. the old G.G. stands like a huge sentinel blocking the way from Wasdale to Borrowdale.

56. Down from Stirrup Crag to Dore Head, the top of its famous (but sick) scree run, then up the N.W. ridge of **Red Pike (Wasdale)**. You will, of course, sit on 'the chair' of rock nearing the summit which is at **166106** and a lofty **2,707ft**. At once a superb vantage point with the prospect of some fine high level walking ahead.

57 - 61. Yes, five in a flash. From Red Pike the route is northwesterly reaching **160114** at **2,760ft** and **Scoat Fell**, highest point (deposit sacks at cairns). Walk the short distance due east, first to **158114** and **2,750ft** to a second top, then a third of a mile towards Haycock and reach **154111** at **2,750 + ft**, the third top. Retrace steps to 158114 and then do the fantastic little 'trip' down to **Steeple (158116) 2,687ft**. This is the sixtieth, perhaps a coming of age in walking a tremendous distance in the sky. From here back to Scoat's highest top at 160114 (sacks) before dropping down and on to **Black Crag** at **164116** and a height of **2,689ft**.

62 & 63. Pillar—perhaps one of the most important names in Lakeland for its famous rock. This is no ordinary place, **the rock is not a place for walkers.** From Black Crag to Wind Gap and up the 500ft on to **Pillar summit 2,927ft (171121)**. Do take a look down over the rock but this tour leaves little time for wandering down to it although it is within the walker's domain to reach the coll beside Pisgah/Pillar. Descend Shamrock Traverse and follow the high level route via Robinson's Cairn to attain **Looking Stead (186118) 2,058ft,** or simply follow the posts down the eastern shoulder to reach the same point. (Robinson's Cairn is a famous landmark. John Wilson Robinson came from Lorton, but I will leave the wonderful inscription to the walker's pleasure on reading it at the cairn).

64 & 65. From Looking Stead continue down to Black Sail pass before tackling the final two tops on this big circuit in the form of **Kirk Fell**. The line of ascent up Kirk is fairly obvious and the cairn at **195105** is not confusing at **2,630ft**. Continue along N.E. direction to reach the second top at **199108** and **2,550 + ft**.

This is the 65th top, all will now be of age, men and women alike!

These last two can be reversed and the descent to Wasdale Head be made via the huge S.W. shoulder which is a 'killer'. I much prefer to drop to Beck Head and descend, to the valley this way for the walk back to the car. Bet you will leave car at Wasdale Head next time whatever you did this time.

13/14 miles; approx. 5,500/6,000ft.

Lakeland peak personified. High Crag, 2,443ft, stands sentinel over Buttermere in early morning sunshine. (Day 7—Top 48)
(Photo: Tom Parker)

Two men and a dog on top of High Stile, 2,644ft. (Day 7—Top 47)
(Photo: Ivor Nicholas)

Great Gable (Day 12—Top 89) rises above the mist-filled valleys as seen from Pillar (Day 9—Top 62). Great End (Day 10—Top 75) is on the right. (Photo: C.D. Gibbons)

On the roof of England. Mountain panorama from near the 3,162ft summit of Scafell (Day 10—Top 68), overlooking Mosedale with Pillar on the right. (Photo: Ivor Nicholas)

The cloud-capped summit of Great Gable broods over Wasdale Head, starting point for Day 10. (Photo: W. Wilkinson)

The classic view of the Langdale Pikes—Harrison Stickle and Pike O' Stickle (Day 14—Tops 111 and 112)—as seen from near Elterwater. (Photo: Noel Habgood)

Winter glory. Whiteside, 2,832ft (Day 20—Top 150) and Helvellyn Low Man as viewed from Raise (Top 149).

The 3,118ft summit of Helvellyn, one of the most frequently climbed of all Lakeland peaks (Top 151). (Photo: G.V. Berry)

The huge and distinctive summit of Catstycam, 2,917ft, with Glenridding Beck in the foreground. (Photo: James E. Tiffin)

The magnificent Striding Edge (Day 21—Top 157), one of the more adventurous routes for the walker. In the distance is the long ridge of High Street (Day 26—Top 199). (Photo: G.V. Berry)

Day 10

Tops 66 - 77 inclusive
Start and finish at Wasdale Head

66.	Slight Side	73 & 74.	Ill Crag
67.	Cam Spout Crag	75.	Great End
68.	Scafell	76.	Esk Pike
69 - 71.	Scafell Pike	77.	Lingmell
72.	Broad Crag		

Schematic/Cartographic Route
(**Warning:** Always consult Ordnance Survey Map, ensure good use of compass).

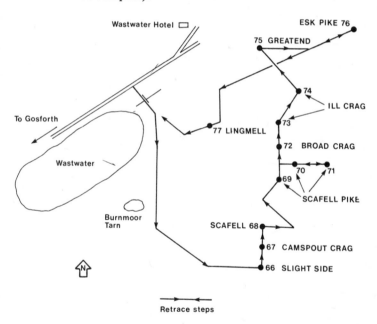

Retrace steps

66. Start and finish at Wasdale Head car park. This is a day to end all days amidst Lakeland's real giants, the Scafells. Leave the camp site and progress in a southerly direction towards Burnmoor Tarn, again this is quite boggy ground. The objective is Slight Side and it is a matter of choice whether to pass Burnmoor and turn up on the Eskdale side over Quagrigg Moss. However, my preference is the more direct, choosing a route over Broad Tongue to attain **Slight Side** at **210050**, an impressive **2,499ft**, although it seems slight indeed with the prospect ahead.

67. The natural route and path now leads on north in awe-inspiring scenery until in a short distance **Cam Spout Crag** is reached at **209059** and **2,850 + ft**.

68. A final battle with the ground brings **Scafell**, the second highest mountain in England. At **207063** and **3,162ft** all of Scafell's height becomes obvious. This is a rugged place, the home of the famous Central Buttress rock which is probably more written about than most other crags. It is easy to look down to Mickledore with a slight tour from the summit. There are four ways (basically) down to Mickledore, (a) via the Lord's Rake, (b) Deep Ghyll and West Wall traverse, (c) Broad Stand and (d) via Foxes Tarn. For the walker, Broad Stand is definitely out and for that matter the condition of Lord's Rake and Deep Ghyll must now deter a recommendation, although they are very direct compared to Foxes Tarn which is the safest route.

69. Leave the Scafell summit cairn and follow the easy ground in a south-easterly direction. Head down to reach a little pond known on most maps as Foxes Tarn. From here it is a large gulley heading downwards but towards the East Buttress. The path from Eskdale is picked up and the unfortunate but safe trudge up to Mickledore is in hand. The Stretcher Box is a solitary reminder to the uninitiated that this is a wild place and serious accidents are not unknown. From here up to **Scafell Pike** is well cairned and relatively easy going; the summit is a notable place at **215072** and **3,210ft**. The highest point in England and a landmark well-fitted to the terrain, it is spectacular. The cairn always reminds me of a tiny crown on such a huge head, for me very impressive.

70 & 71. Head N.E. and down to the coll before Broad Crag; at this point a detour is essential to get all the tops as it were. The south-westerly descent into Little Narrowcore is to pick up in either order **221068 at 2,500 + ft** and **220069 at 2,500ft**.

72. When back on the coll it is up on to **Broad Crag** itself for the next summit at **219076**, a huge **3,054ft** (the same height as Skiddaw, but only on this list classed a separate top).

73 & 74. Ill Crag is yet another extension of 'The Pikes' and here it is afforded two distinctive tops. At **223075** it is **3,040ft** (another lofty partner in the pedantic search for 3,000 footers). Further across to reach **224079** and **2,950 + ft** is the second effort, a lesser height.

I must be forgiven for going through this area so quickly, but this is the way of basic tours—and this is a route plan rather than a guide.

75. Down a little following the cairns and up the 200/300 ft on to **Great End**. Well-named, it drops in nearly all directions from this point. At the summit at **227084** and **2,984ft** quite a place—the views over towards Great Gable are excellent.

76. Then perhaps my only dirty trick of the day is to slog back down towards the true Esk Hause; either retrace the steps south or head south-east over a little craggy route. From the Hause (234080) head up the south-east shoulder to 'bag' Esk Pike. For me a lonely spot, but well trod I fancy by the worn path. The view down Eskdale and the flanks of the Scafells is unsurpassed here. **Esk Pike** top is **237075** at **2,903ft**, a well lofted place.

77. Now back to Esk Hause and then up to the coll between Ill Crag and Great End, descending to Round How and the corridor route (always assuming that no-one fancies Styhead first or going over Ill Crag and Broad Crag again). The corridor route is picked up here and followed to the head of the huge slash called Piers Gill; here we leave the Scafell route and head N.W. up onto **Lingmell** at **209082** and **2,649ft**, no mean hill. This truly fantastic top has got the lot; its views to Great Gable and the Scafells are superb and the view down into Piers Gill is enough to make most people's hair stand on end!

The walk down to Wasdale Head will be slow for if you're not completely jiggered, you should be well-worn or 'fagged out' to use a printable expression.

15/16 miles; approx. 6,000ft of ascent.

Day 11

Tops 78 - 86 inclusive

Start and finish at Seathwaite

78 & 79. Seathwaite Fell	84 & 85. Glaramara
80 - 83. Allan Crags	86. Cam Crag

Schematic/Cartographic Route

(Warning: Always consult Ordnance Survey Map, ensure good use of compass).

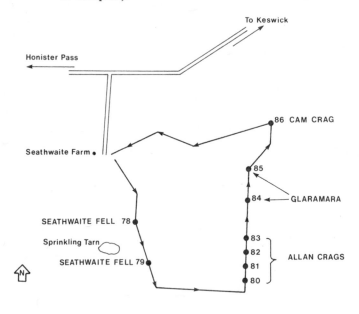

78 & 79. Start and finish near Seathwaite Village. Head up the valley, follow Grains Gill and Stockley Bridge, take off right and follow cairned path on to **Seathwaite Fell** at 1,970ft. This is a natural top but further ahead there lies two points at the required height. At **227095** and **2,025 + ft** lies the first and on a contour taking us south of Sprinkling Tarn is **230093**, another **2,000ft** point.

80.   Continuing in S.W. direction to Broad Coll where the shelter is; however, this is not Esk Hause which is higher up. From this point it is a N.E. turn up the 200/300ft to the summit of **Allan Crags (237085) 2,572ft.**

81 - 83. The ridge generally heads N.E. and on its way to Glaramara, it picks up three tops on this very interesting walk, **(241092) 2,200 + ft, (243097) 2,350 + ft** and finally **(246102) 2,550 + ft.**

84 - 86. Glaramara is indeed an immense hill of considerable interest; hidden little tarns, crags, little valleys, it's got the lot. **Glaramara summit (247106) 2,560ft** is a pleasant place but in mist it can be a strange hill. It is important not to follow the main path down to Seathwaite, instead head for the cairn at **250108** and at **2,300ft.** This has a grand view towards Seatoller. From this point, called Comb Head, turn right or east down to Coomb Door and follow on N.E. to **Cam Crag (256114) 2,000ft + .** This area is very beautiful and a joy to wander in at the end of a good day. A choice can be made yet again with a drop into Stonethwaite or the shorter walk down Comb Gill—a little care is needed here, but no real problems. However, it is better kept for a summer's day with good views to enjoy the real splendour of the place. In mist it can be confusing to say the least, but so much is lost without a clear view when walking the tops on any journey.

9/10 miles; approx. 2,750ft of ascent.

Day 12

Tops 87 - 94 inclusive

Start and finish at Seathwaite

87.	Base Brown	90.	Brandreth
88.	Green Gable	91.	Grey Knotts
89.	Great Gable	92-94.	Fleetwith Pike

Schematic/Cartographic Route

(**Warning:** Always consult Ordnance Survey Map, ensure good use of compass).

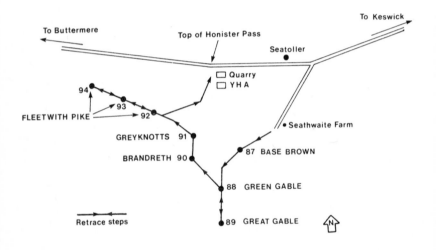

87. Start and finish near Seathwaite Village. It is a straight-forward start through the farmhouse bridge and right, straight up Sour Milk Gill past the 'hanging stone', a strange geological freak, and up to the summit of **Base Brown (225114) 2,120ft.**

88. Continue S.W. up this huge shoulder and join the main G.G. path and reach **Green Gable (215107) 2,603ft.**

89. Descend into Windy Gap and up the enormous hulk of **Great Gable (G.G.).** So big is the hill and so popular that the Gable girth is regarded, rightly so, as a fine day out. However, the summit is reached at **211103** and **2,949ft**, though it deserves to

46

be a 3,000 footer. No visitor should forget to pop down to the Westmoreland Cairn and view the postage stamp fields of Wasdale Head. 'Tis a sheer delight and Scottish in its magnitude.

90. Now we have to retrace ground all the way to Green Gable and head generally north for just about 1 mile to attain **Brandreth Top (215119) 2,344ft.**

91. This is merely ½ mile or so in N.E. direction and **Grey Knotts** is reached at **219126** and **2,287ft.** This is a strange and interesting place with lots of little tops and hidden valleys, a delight on a summer day when most will by-pass the place en-route for Great Gable.

92 - 94. Heading north the quarry workings are reached, and then up N.W. on to **Fleetwith.** Keep the huge drop down to Honister Pass well to the right. Honister Crags are really tremendous, but very dangerous. At **213141** and **2,050ft,** we reach the first top then a little further along the crag line **211141,** again at **2,050ft,** and finally the main top at **206142** and **2,126ft.**

On the morning of my 35th birthday I recall taking my 6-year old son up from Gatesgarth. We were on the top for 9.30 a.m.—the young man never gave up that day!

From Fleetwith top it's back along the ridge, picking an easy route back to the quarries and then down to the Youth Hostel and a walk down the road (or a lift) to Seatoller and then Seathwaite.

11/12 miles; approx. 4,000ft of ascent.

Day 13

Tops 95 - 108 inclusive

Start and finish at Dungeon Ghyll Hotel, Langdale

95.	Tongue Head	105.	Red How
96-98.	Bowfell	106.	The Knott
99.	Shelter Crag	107.	Cold Pike
100-104.	Crinkle Crags	108.	Pike o' Blisco

Schematic/Cartographic Route

(**Warning:** Always consult Ordnance Survey Map, ensure good use
of compass).

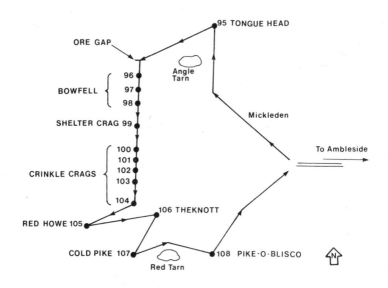

95.   To begin walk into Mickleden and then up into Rosset
Gill, keep to the path that passes by Angle Tarn and walk
up to the small dome known as **Tongue Head (241080) 2,250ft**. The
main interest here is the commanding view afforded of Langstrath.

96 - 98. Up onto Ore Gap from Tongue Head, turning then onto
Bowfell, heading generally south, at **245069** and **2,825ft**,
the first of three tops is reached. A short circuit fetches up the
second top at **245067** and **2,850ft**. The third and highest point is
found at **245064** and **2,960ft**. It is not hard to understand why many

people go into raptures about Bowfell, since it is a really magnificent mountain in most aspects. Huge crags adorn the sides and the summit is truly a pleasant place to be. Care is needed in mist but the routes off are usually well worn.

99 - 104. From Bowfell we descend to the Three Tarns which is the lowest ground between the latter and the next objectives, Shelter Crag and Crinkle Crags. The ridge needs little explanation with Langdale to the left (east) and Eskdale to the right (west). **Shelter Crag** is attained at **249054** and **2,650ft**. From here the ramble is not too severe until the first of the **Crinkles** is attained at **249052** and **2,680ft**. The next three are straightforward at **249051** and **2,730ft, 249050** and **2,740ft** and the highest point at **248049** and **2,816ft**. To reach the final Crinkle is a much larger gap but this is found at **250046** and **2,733ft**. The whole area is outstanding; like Bowfell it is a splendid place to be, an airy turret of considerable character. The views are never lacking and are particularly good towards the Scafells.

105. Having achieved six tops in the space of one major fell we must now settle down to the singular objective which is next **Red How**. The walk is interesting and easy going, heading over to the topmost reaches of the Duddon Valley. At **251034** and **2,426ft**, the cairn is found. This is a pleasant place, all the more so since it appears to be rarely visited; not the well trodden path over the Crinkles—but a mere track here.

106. Our next objective is somewhat awkward since it necessitates retracing part of the path and holding height; however it is not complicated except in mist, then it needs care. **The Knott** at **260043** and **2,200ft** is an odd place; one which hardly ranks with the remainder of the day but, nevertheless on the list.

107. A gentle, agreeable stroll for half a mile or so brings **Cold Pike** at **264035** and **2,259ft**. This is a fine vantage point for looking towards the Conistons and adjacent high ground. Red Tarn below is especially pleasant to look down to; again this is not a popular location.

108. To reach **Pike o'Blisco** can be done various ways, but it is probably easier to retrace the path taken from top 107 and then head down towards the low ground between Cold Pike and our last (for today) objective. The way up is obvious but I like to use the splendid rocky outcrops that make the ascent of interest, which at this stage of the day is useful. The summit is a fine place, well on the beaten track as it were, at **271042** and **2,304ft**.

For one day fourteen 'tops' is no mean achievement; however one must not forget that some were easier than others. The descent can be several ways, but I imagine most people will be content to take the shortest route which probably is Wall End. This will rank a grand day in almost any calendar. Fine weather is good for appreciating the terrain and views, but not essential if care is taken and prudent use of map reading technique followed.

12/13 miles approx. 5,000ft of ascent.

Day 14

Tops 109-113 inclusive

Start and finish at Langdale

109 & 110. Thunacar Knott 112. Pike O' Stickle
111. Harrison Stickle 113. Rossett Pike

Schematic/Cartographic Route

(**Warning:** Always consult Ordnance Survey Map, ensure good use
of compass).

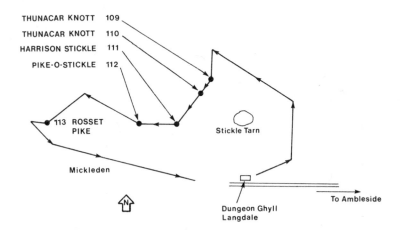

109 & 110. Start and finish at Dungeon Ghyll, Langdale. Follow
the main route to Stickle Tarn, pass the tarn on its
east side path, continue turning west and join the ridge between High
Raise and **Thunacar Knott** at or near 280086. Then turn due south
and reach the first of the tops at **279081** and **2,351ft**; it is easy going
to the second top at **279079** and **2,362ft**, the main top. This hill is
more frequently called Pavey Arc and its famous walkers' traverse
of Jack's Rake is quite something. However, more time to bother
with that later (if you must).

111. To **Harrison Stickle** (as we are here in the Langdale
Pikes) is indeed a joyful walk and interesting on the
summit at the point **282073** and **2,403ft**. The top is a fine place with
commanding views all round.

51

112.   Along generally N.E. there is the next pike in the form of
Pike O' Stickle, a grand 'airy' place to be perched in
summer. This is reached with a little scramble at **274074** and **2,323ft.**

113.   From Pike O' Stickle our next objective is some two miles
distant. First N.W. and then S.W. over Mart Crag Moor,
Stake Pass and Langdale Coomb heading for **Rossett Pike** at **250075**
and **2,106ft,** quite a landmark at the head of Mickledore. From here
it's down Rossett Gill to the car.

Perhaps one of the easier days in good autumn weather, when the
tops are a joy and not to be rushed. Try to glimpse the 'hard men'
on Gimmer; it's hilarious that they seem to stand perched for hours
and while we have traversed several miles they rise a few
hundred feet. I'll be honest, I haven't the guts, but no doubt some
will want to argue about that.

9/10 miles; approx. 2,500ft of ascent.

Day 15

Top 114

Start and finish at Eskdale

114.   Harter Fell

Schematic/Cartographic Route

(**Warning:** Always consult Ordnance Survey Map, ensure good use of compass).

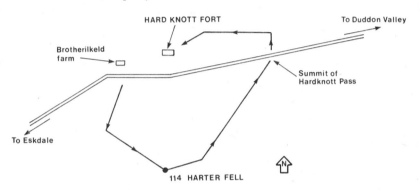

114.   Start and finish at Brotherilkeld. This is the one and only one-top day and perhaps it is reasonable. For although there is little to add on to Harter Fell, naturally it is reasonable to visit Hard Knott and its fort of Roman origin. From the car park it is possible to cross the beck and head S.W. until 207003, then turn S.E. and east to the summit of **Harter Fell** at **218997** and **2,140ft.** It is a beautiful fell from Eskdale and especially nice to be on it; the interesting little outcrops are pleasant and the views towards the Scafells magnificent.

Heading N.E. the gentle slopes bring the top of Hard Knott pass and if you haven't fallen over yourself watching the antics of motorists by now, then the earnest look on the faces of those drivers who pass you at this point should make your day. In summer it really can be comical, although I must admit I don't really care for it much at any time.

Across the road and up on to Hard Knott at **231014**, a superb vantage point. The descent past the fort is interesting and a good short day will have been enjoyed.

5 miles and approx. 2,500ft.

Day 16
Tops 115 - 126 inclusive
Start and finish at Wrynose Pass

115.	Great Carrs	121.	Coniston Old Man
116.	Grey Friar	122.	Brim Fell
117.	Dow Crag	123.	Swirl How
119 & 120.	Walna Scar	124-126.	Wetherlam

Schematic/Cartographic Route

(**Warning:** Always consult Ordnance Survey Map, ensure good use of compass).

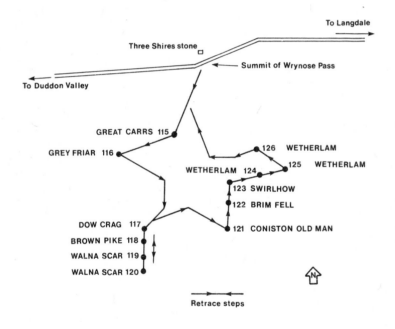

115.   Start and finish on Wrynose Pass summit. Since the objective is to 'do' all the Coniston tops in the day, a start at 1,280ft is very welcome and an advantage. Leave the road heading up the ridge you reach Little Carrs and then **Great Carrs** at **270010** and **2,575ft**.

116. Leave Great Carrs in a S.W. direction and stride out until **Grey Friar** is reached at **260004** and **2,536ft.**

117 - 120. Leave Grey Friar and join the M1 to Coniston Old Man before 'sliding off', keeping as low as possible on Brim Fell and then over Goats Hause to attain the superb **Dow Crag** at **263978** and **2,555ft.** Goats Water just below looks really good. Continue over and heading south to reach **Brown Pike** at **261966** and **2,237ft.** Very slightly west from the south line attain the two outcrops of **Walna Scar** at **258964** and **2,000ft+** first and then **254957** and **2,000ft+**.

121. It is necessarily a hard slog back now over Brown Pike and Dow Crag to Goats Hause, then up on to the **Old Man of Coniston** at **272978** and **2,635ft**, the highest point in the area.

122 & 123. Head off north now and continue over the first rise of **Brim Fell** at **271986** and **2,611ft**, a rounded top, and then reach the central mass of **Swirl How** at **273005** and **2,630ft.** Just a little less than the height of the 'Old Man' but infinitely more attractive.

124 - 126. Take off due west (almost) down the excellent Prison Band—looking right to Levers Water way below. Progress to the bottom of the Prison Band, follow a line to the east side of **Wetherlam** and then to reach **283008** and **2,400ft+**. From this point it is a choice but I feel the **289008** is best got at **2,400ft+** before walking on to the main top at **288011** and **2,502ft.**

From here the walk back is unfortunately a long one and for this reason this should be left for a 10 hour day in good weather with plenty of fodder. I suggest a descent into Tilberthwaite and skirt round, trying to hold as much height as possible, picking up Wet Side edge and top of Wrynose at 1,280ft and a car. A demanding day but a good one.

16/17 miles; approx. 4,500/5,000ft of ascent

Day 17

Tops 127 - 129 inclusive

Start and finish at Dunmail Raise

127. Ullscarf
128. High Raise

129. Sargeant Man

Schematic/Cartographic Route

(**Warning:** Always consult Ordnance Survey Map, ensure good use of compass).

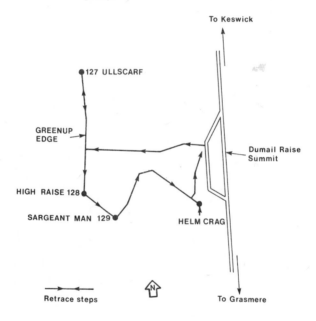

127.   Start and finish from the summit of Dunmail Raise.
There is little doubt that your initial scan of this proposed route will make you wonder, but nevertheless I commend it to you. Leave that bouldery pile which reputedly covers that deceased manifestation of royalty, and head due west up the rough edge of Steel Fell. It seems arduous but in fact with steady plodding it is not bad. The relationship with motor cars in reality fades when the crest is reached and Steel Fell top appears a little way off at

320111 approx. From Steel Fell top, a grand viewpoint, the route is apparent; it twists and winds its way gently towards Greenup Edge which is the target initially. At 295102 approx. the bridleway from Grasmere to Borrowdale should be encountered and it is from this that Greenup Edge is attained at 285104 approx. Here we alter our direction from westerly to almost north, and achieve our first top of **Ullscarf** at **292122** and **2,370ft.**

128. Leave Ullscarf by the same route and continue over the ground which is rolling but not rugged at this level. Within 1½ miles or so you get to **High Raise** at **281095** and **2,500ft.** I recall two things about this place: (1) I saw the Golden Eagle nearby and (2) a young couple back-packing with a tiny baby heading off late evening towards Langstrath; somehow this touched me greatly.

129. **Sargeant Man,** a surprising little top, is very near at **286089** and **2,414ft.** It has a good view towards the Windermere area.

From this perch it is possible to cut down towards Wythburn without touching our conquests, and by skirting east of Ash Crags— there is a path of sorts—eventually we rejoin the bridleway from Grasmere at or near 295102. A little way down at 297101 approx., take off left (north-east) towards Calf Crag, then follow the ridge all the way over Pike of Carrs and Gibson Knott until Helm Crag is reached. Go up Helm Crag, for like me, I'm sure you may wonder what all the fuss is about when people relate to the Lion and Lamb. Return to the coll and choose your own way back to Dunmail. I personally gained height and skirted the 900 foot mark to avoid the horrid bog that surrounds Raise Beck here.

A true tour and three tops to boot.

10/11 miles; approx. 3,000/3,500ft of ascent.

Day 18

Tops 130 - 138 inclusive

Start and finish at Dunmail Raise

130. Seat Sandal
131. Fairfield
132. Greatrigg Man

133 - 136. Rydal Fell
137. Erne Crag
138. Heron Pike

Schematic/Cartographic Route

(**Warning:** Always consult Ordnance Survey Map, ensure good use of compass).

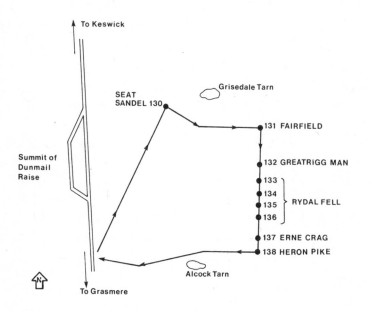

130. Well down Dunmail Raise start and finish 337091 approx. Park nearby. Turn up at Mill Bridge and work out the way on to South Ridge of **Seat Sandal;** constant attention is required to keep optimum height and not waste energy. The top of Seat Sandal is an interesting place for me—often missed out by the high hill men—but I like the place. At **344115** and **2,415ft** the summit is found well cairned and it is a joy to watch all the dots of people on Fairfield and Helvellyn.

131. In fact we will go to **Fairfield** on this tour. Dropping down towards the Grisedale Hause is fairly steep; follow the wall but veer north before the bottom. The walk up Fairfield is never in doubt; it is a plod but the glimpses of the tarn are a pleasant consideration as you sweat it out. The top at **358117** is at a respectable **2,863ft**, the highest eastern part of Lakeland. It commands attention, for the views into Grisedale and Deepdale are unsurpassed and the prospect of Striding Edge lies not too far away.

132. Down south towards **Greatrigg Man** is an undulating stroll; it quite lacks the rugged grandeur of Fairfield's top but is pleasant enough with Windermere in the distance. At **356104** the top is reached at **2,513ft**.

133 - 138. My Goodness this is good stuff, the pedantic illusion evaporates by the stride of the wetted boot. This ridge is pleasant and the tops soon fall like toy soldiers when the door blows open. First we cross **356095** at **2,000ft +**, then **356093** at **2,000ft +**, **356092, 2,022ft**, the topmost, then to **356091** at **2,000 ft**. (bit repetitive this jargon), all on **Rydal Fell**. With a deviation at **357087** the **2,000ft + Erne Crag** is reached and finally **Heron Pike** (**355083**)**2,003ft**. Perhaps the centrality in relation to the tourist trade makes forgiveness easy for these last five points in the sky seem insignificant—although of course its related to contours.

The descent from Heron Pike is sharp but Alcock Tarn and the higher opulence of Grasmere can be pleasant. Certainly Wordsworth thought so, but who is he but a normal human of extraordinary good luck. To be listened to in your own life is rare, but he had his failings. After objecting to the railway extension he reputedly invested in its fortunes—a true soul or a realist.

8/10 miles; approx. 3,500ft. of ascent.

Day 19
Tops 139 - 144 inclusive

Start and finish at St Johns in the Vale

139. Clough Head   142.   Great Dodd
140. Calfhow Pike   143 & 144. Stybarrow
141. Randerside

Schematic/Cartographic Route

(Warning: **Always consult Ordnance Survey Map, ensure good use of compass).**

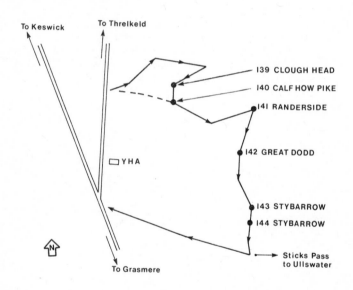

139.   Start and finish at St. John's in the Vale. You can park almost anywhere along this road, that is because I anticipate some road work in any event. However, the small car park at nearby Lowthwaite Farm seems quite convenient. Pick up the old coach road for a short distance and then turn up to Threlkeld Knotts; this is a very impressive place with level ground between the walker and the face of Clough Head. It is possible to continue east and pick up White Pike at 338230 reference approx., but

alternatively leave the huge amphitheatre and head S.W. towards the top of Wanthwaite Crags and finally to the summit which is certainly the shorter way. At **Clough Head** compass point **334225** and **2,381ft,** the view is extensive, quite visibly the end of a ridge. You effectively turn your back on life here and head for the high ground.

140.   Our next point is **Calfhow Pike,** which is little more than a rocky outcrop but strangely can be picked out easily from a distance. At **330211** and **2,166 ft** it is an odd summit to say the least.

141 & 142. The stroll to Great Dodd should be interrupted by a contour movement around the upper reaches of Mosedale Beck, heading for and achieving with little problem **Randerside** at **349211** and **2,250ft.** The view down into the extensive Deepdale below is truly surprising and a grand area for an overcast drizzly day—exploration ground. From this point trudge back up the south-west edge of **Great Dodd** and at **342204** and **2,807ft** this huge top is reached.

143 & 144. Now we move off S.W. to reach Watson's Dodd at, 2,584ft, favoured by some guide books as a summit but not by this list of tops. It seems the physical/geological qualifications are not found here so we can skirt round it and head S.E. at this point to reach **Stybarrow Dodd** at **343189** and **2,750 + ft** first, and then turning S.W. again to reach the second top at **341186** and **2,756ft** (the true top of the fell).

Moving over the summit and down to join Sticks Pass is easy and the following section down to Legburthwaite is a pleasant walk, and then back to the car. On a good day many will reverse the ridge missing out Randerside and dropping off towards the car at Calfhow Pike, descending to the sheepfold and then keeping south of Beckthorns Gill to Fornside.

11/12 miles; approximately 3,000ft of ascent.

Day 20
Tops 145 - 152 inclusive
Start and finish at Glenridding

145.	Sheffield Pike	150.	Whiteside
146 & 147.	Hartside	151.	Helvellyn
148.	Greenside	152.	Catstycam
149.	Raise		

Schematic/Cartographic Route

(**Warning:** Always consult Ordnance Survey Map, ensure good use of compass).

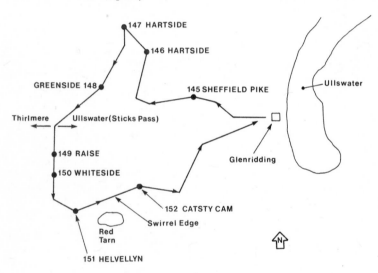

145. Start and finish in Glenridding at the car park. Glenridding always holds something special for me, a once industrial oasis amidst such magnificent scenery. Admittedly the tourist scene is evident, but to walk, or better still to stay, at Greenside is different to most other places in Lakeland. To start the day, stroll up the mine path past the Travellers Rest and follow on towards the Youth Hostel. Two elevated rows of cottages, 'Rawhead', appear; pass these and at approximately 379171 turn north up the steep grassy bank. (There is a sort of path). Head for the coll west of Glenridding Dodd (378174); the detour on to the Dodd is a superb interlude with magnificent views of Ullswater. Now proceed up the south-east ridge of Sheffield Pike which is usually slow since the views around are interesting. On reaching **369182** and **2,232ft, Sheffield Pike** is achieved.

146 - 148. The way to the appropriately named Greenside is not too difficult, crossing Nick Head at about 1,800ft. However, to save time on our tour it is perhaps best to contour above the Eastern Crags which circle the head of Glencoyne. Top 146 is reached at Hartside's first top, **362195** and **2,350 + ft.** The second top is at **359197** and the highest point at **2,481ft.** The southerly trek is always at high level and **Greenside** is reached at **353187** and **2,600 + ft.** Quite a rounded rambling summit with little of interest.

149. The route to Sticks Pass is optional; one can go over Stybarrow or a more direct way. From Sticks Pass go up on to the summit of **Raise** at **343174** and **2,889ft.** This now brings the main Helvellyn ridge into view.

150 & 151. Continuing along this magnificent ridge towards Helvellyn the views are superb. The first high spot is **Whiteside** at **338166** and **2,832ft.** From here the walk gets even more spectacular with the view of Catstycam on the left and Brown Cove Crags on the right. The summit of **Helvellyn** is frequently like Blackpool Promenade in summer, but they are getting good exercise, so what is there to worry about. This then is the summit at **341151** and **3,118ft.** This is the fourth and final of the real three thousand footers in Lakeland. I think there can be little argument: though the views elsewhere can be better, the sight of Red Tarn, Striding Edge and Catstycam form a grand mountain scene.

152. Slightly north of the summit cairn the route we will take is very rugged but reasonably safe in the form of Swirrel Edge towards Catstycam itself. Care is needed but there are no real difficulties for the average fell walker. When reaching the low ground preceding our objective the main path down to Red Tarn is apparent. **Catstycam** at **348158** and **2,917ft** is a huge, distinctive summit and perhaps the most satisfying vantage point for peacefully viewing the surrounding terrain. I recall vividly a crisp clear October morning when I first visited this place with no one, not even a bird, to share the experience with.

From the summit one can retreat to the path previously mentioned that leads to Red Tarn or over the north-west shoulder and down to Greenside Y.H.A. and Glenridding.

14/15 miles; approximately 4,500-5,000ft of ascent.

Day 21

Tops 153 - 162 inclusive

Start and finish at Patterdale

153 - 156.	Birkhouse Moor	160.	Dollywagon Pike
157.	Striding Edge	161.	St. Sunday Crag
158.	Nethermost Pike	162.	Birks
159.	High Crag		

Schematic/Cartographic Route

(**Warning:** Always consult Ordnance Survey Map, ensure good use of compass).

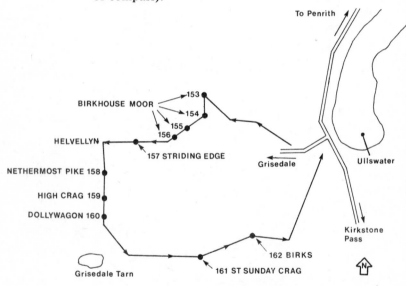

153 - 156. Start and finish in Patterdale at **390161** or at the nearest parking area. The prospect of the finest ridge available for the pedestrian is indeed daunting but the beginning is more ordinary and tiresome. Birkhouse Moor is afforded four tops. At any convenient point leave the main path to Striding Edge and go directly north to join the wall that descends direct to Keldas and then follow on upwards to the high ground. This summit is then an exercise in map reading, which in mist can be a positive nightmare. First, however, leave the wall and pick out **365163**, and here at **2,318ft** the first top is reached with views towards Greenside. Then turn south to reach **363159** and **2,350 + ft** (the highest point), go back to the wall and **361158** and **2,300 + ft** is the third top, finally reaching the fourth previously referred to of **Birkhouse's** tops at **360157** and **2,300ft**.

157. Now with the map reading exercise finished it's off to the big stuff, and the M1 to Striding Edge. At the outset the magnificence of this route is not apparent, but a knife edge suddenly emerges upturned to slice into the odd posterior here and there. There are only one or two awkward places on the ridge and with due care there is little to worry about—**but like many of the routes this can be a serious undertaking in winter.** The area of Helvellyn has probably claimed more lives than the rest of Lakeland; therefore, care is vital. The summit of **Striding Edge** is at **351149** and **2,832ft.** On the summit of Helvellyn itself (a top not in this tour) turn south towards the next point.

158 - 160. This is a fine 'airy' length of crag which faces generally east with the huge cove and Grisedale below. In ¾ mile you reach **Nethermost Pike** at **344141** and **2,920ft.** Continuing the line but leaving the main path you reach **High Crag** at **343136** and **2,850ft.** The next top 160 is the comical sounding **Dollywagon Pike** at **346130** and **2,810ft.** From here the very beautiful tarn of Grisedale comes into view and it is a treat to pause at its eastern edges, viewing those heading up on to Helvellyn or Fairfield —a busy place since Dunmail Raise summit is only a half hour away.

161. The map needs attention now and a little care should allow one to pick up the path which leads on to St. Sunday Crag, i.e. direct to Deepdale Hause. This is now a fairly gentle stroll but after the ground already covered, perhaps it will be something of a relief on reaching the summit of **St. Sunday Crag** at **369134** and **2,756ft.** This is a splendid place to spend a few minutes before setting off for the final top of the day.

162. Now head off in a north-easterly direction continuing the fairly level but dull trudge to **Birks** at **382145** and **2,040ft**, not a particularly interesting place.

From Birks it is really up to you, but the best way is probably south-west and picking up the upper reaches of Hagbeck and Glemara Park.

14/15 miles; approximately 4,000ft of ascent.

Day 22

Tops 163 - 167 inclusive

Start and finish at North end Kirkstone Pass

163. Hart Crag	165 & 166. Little Hart Crag
164. Dove Crag	167. Raven Crag

Schematic/Cartographic Route

(**Warning:** Always consult Ordnance Survey Map, ensure good use of compass).

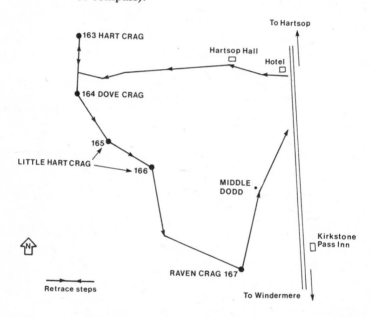

163.   Start and finish at the foot of Kirkstone Pass in a suitable lay-by. Set off across the valley bottom towards Hartsop Hall at 398120. From here a winding, rising but restful path leads up the valley, passing the Stangs on the left and circling into Hunsett Cove. From here our objective is Hart Crag which can be attained by heading up north of Dove Crag and turning north to attain the summit of **Hart Crag** at **369112** and **2,698ft**. Dovedale is a pleasant place to be on a nice day and a relatively easy undertaking until the last short section.

66

164.   Set off back down in an approximately S.W. direction and up on to the easily obtainable **Dove Crag** at **374104** and **2,603ft**. The ruggedness of Dove Crag itself is by no means apparent at the summit cairn, but the ascent via Dovedale will have made the walker aware of its size.

165 & 166.   From Dove Crag the route is obvious but to reach 165 top head off in an easterly direction to a knoll of sorts at **384101** where **Little Hart Crag** is reached at **2,000 + ft**. Leave here in a southerly direction to reach the second of these minor Hart Crag tops at **387100** and **2,091ft**. This latter location is a superb stopping place with a magnificent view down into Dovedale and back towards Hartsop Hall in the distance.

167.   Then walk across Scandale Pass keeping as much height as possible and picking up the path on to **Raven Crag*** which is reached at **396087** and **2,541ft**. You should wander a little to the south and observe the activity on the summit of Kirkstone Pass from various points. Thirsty work this, and the bar of the inn is an attractive proposition. However, we now have to regain the lower end of Kirkstone Pass and the road is a laborious and uninteresting walk; therefore, leave the top over the Red Screes and continue north over Middle Dodd which is a grand vantage point, before dropping off the high ground nearer the foot of the pass.

Perhaps not the longest of day's walking but a reasonable route indeed.

10/11 miles; approximately 4,000ft of ascent.

* or Red Screes.

Day 23

Start and finish at Hartsop

168.	Hartsop Dodd	172.	Froswick
169.	John Bell's Banner	173.	Ill Bell
170.	Stoney Cove Pike	174.	Yoke
171.	Thornthwaite Crag	175 - 177.	Grey Crag

Schematic/Cartographic Route

(**Warning:** Always consult Ordnance Survey Map, ensure good use of compass).

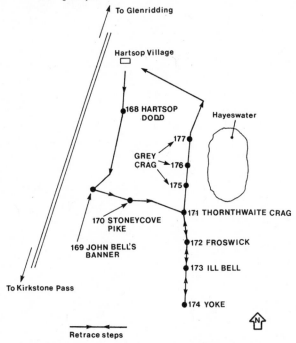

168.   Start and finish in Hartsop village east car park. The prospect here is a good day beginning with a hard slog up on to **Hartsop Dodd.** The direct northern slopes are steep, but it is a very direct route to the summit at **411118** and **2,018ft**. The view from here is excellent, particularly towards Helvellyn.

169 & 170. The going is more leisurely now, gently rising towards Cauldale Moor or as it is generally known Stoney Cove Pike. Before attaining the top at **413100** and **2,474ft** there is **John Bell's Banner.** Look for the tiny cross mounted here quite near to the summit. Now head back towards the summit of **Stoney Cove Pike** itself at **418100** and **2,502ft** which is the highest point in the immediate area.

171. The next objective necessitates a long drop to the mouth of Threshthwaite and upwards to the distinctive landmark which is found on **Thornthwaite Crag** summit at **431100** and **2,569ft.** I always find this a marvellous resting place very much a crossroads in the hills.

172. Due south in a relatively short distance we reach **Froswick** at the lesser but nevertheless impressive height of **2,359ft** on a reference of **435085.**

173. Continue almost due south along this huge spur and reach **Ill Bell** at **436077** and **2,476ft.** A somewhat surprising place, very airy.

174. The most southerly point of the day brings up the oddly named summit of **Yoke** at **438067** and **2,309ft.** Now I am afraid it is back to Thornthwaite Crag; the walking is good but Ill Bell will make even the best curse a little. Once back on Thornthwaite Crag if you are human you will want some refreshment.

175 - 177. This gentle ridge is a joy at this time of day and Hayeswater to the right will occupy the eye as much as the huge Helvellyn in the distance. The first top at **429110** and **2,331ft** is the highest point of **Grey Crag** and the second point at **428114** and **2,286ft** is something of an anti-climax. Finally, the last top of the day is reached at **426118** and **2,250ft.** This is a tremendous view so late in the day. It only remains now to drop over the end of Grey Crag to pick up the Hayeswater/Hartsop path and the stroll back— after something of a gruelling day.

12/13 miles; approximately 5,000ft of ascent.

Day 24

Tops 178 - 188 inclusive

Start and finish at Hartsop

178.	Rest Dodd	183.	Red Crag
179.	The Knott	184 & 185.	Wether Hill
180.	Ramps Gill Head	186.	Loadpot Hill
181.	High Row	187.	Place Fell
182.	Raven Howe	188.	Round Howe

Schematic/Cartographic Route

(**Warning:** Always consult Ordnance Survey Map, ensure good use of compass).

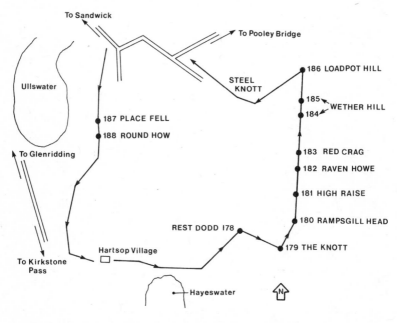

178. Start and finish in Hartsop village. Set off along the rambling path towards Hayeswater gaining height gradually until the small dam is reached. Our first objective lies due north of Hayeswater but a direct route would prove to be rather tedious. It is easier to leave the northern shores and at approx.

433129 head northwards up the slopes of **Rest Dodd**. At **432136** and **2,278ft** the top is attained, not a particularly inspiring place.

179.   Leaving Rest Dodd head south and in a short distance you reach an equally uninteresting point at **437127** and **2,423ft** called **The Knott**.

180.   Suddenly the view improves as height is gained moving up on to **Rampsgill Head**. This is a good place to be with plenty to interest the rambler. The summit is found at **444128** and **2,581ft**; the nearby crags are a fine ending to the valley they head.

181 - 185.   (When you walk this route this lumping together will be accepted). The journey to Loadpot Hill is a long one and the section from Rampsgill Head to High Raise sets the scene for a bit of a drag. The summit of **High Raise** is reached at **448134** and **2,634ft**. Further along the ridge we reach **Raven Howe** at **450144** and **2,358ft**. Now it is just a case of gritting your teeth and pressing on until reaching **Red Crag (450153) 2,328ft**. Our next objective is **Wether Hill**; finding the summit here is a little difficult. The first top is at **455163** and **2,210ft**, the second at **456167** and **2,200ft**. Neither will cause much excitement but at least 186 top is clearly visible.

186.   **Loadpot Hill** is a pleasing arrival and something of a change with a ruin quite near to the cairn; the summit is reached at **457181** and **2,201ft**.

187 & 188.   Now for some harder work. From the previous top there is a choice of sorts; either head off N.W. and down towards Howtown via Fusedale or perhaps the more attractive way is to skirt round the head of the valley past the ruin and on to Steel Knotts, picking up the path that leads to the old church at 433183. After the somewhat tiring ridge the road will be a welcome change heading for Sandwick, taking a short cut to the foot of Sleet Fell. The remainder of this is a real test of stamina; at approx. 425193 it's a push up the slopes of the magnificent **Place Fell**. This is splendid walking with good views of Ullswater on the right. The summit is attained at **405169** and **2,154ft**. This top holds something special for me—it was here that I personally completed the 2,000 footers. Now it's nearly all downhill. **Round Howe** is the last top on what will probably have been a very hard day; this is a mere mound compared with what has gone before. The top is found at **409166** and **2,000ft**.

For the really super fit, Angletarn Crags stands between you and the car, but for most it will be the track from Boredale Hause to Hartsop village which is a real delight in good weather.

Quite a day!

15/16 miles; approx. 5,000ft of ascent.

Day 25

Tops 189 - 197 inclusive

Start and finish at Haweswater

189.	Selside Pike	194.	Kentmere Pike
190 & 191.	Branstree	195.	Brown Howe
192.	Tarn Crag	196.	Harter Fell
193.	Grey Crag	197.	Adam Seat

Schematic/Cartographic Route

(**Warning:** Always consult Ordnance Survey Map, ensure good use of compass).

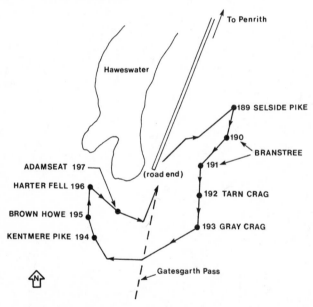

189.　　Start and finish at Haweswater. The drive alongside this large man-made water mass is indeed rather pleasant, the road ending where it is proposed to commence this the penultimate day of my grand tour. There have been many critics of the water schemes in Lakeland but I always enjoy a visit to Mardale Head; perhaps it would be different had I seen the valley as it originally used to be. Parking at 469107, leave the car and set off up in the general direction of Selside Pike. This is rather awkward but with a

72

little reasoning a line can be selected after the initial few hundred feet or so heading up towards Branstree. At 480110 it is possible to follow round to our objective, first heading S.E. then N.E., reaching **Selside Pike** at **491112** and **2,142ft**. This is not the best approach to the hill, a much better and more attractive way leads in from Swindale.

190 & 191. Moving off south-east for **Branstree**, consult the map and carefully select the best way to attain the first top at **487103** and **2,200ft**. Pass the post and press on to reach Arkle Crag Pike at **478100** and **2,333ft**. This is the second top of Branstree. The view over to High Street (my 199th top) is impressive and a lonely one, since you won't meet many on this hill!

192. Now its S.E. over one of Lakeland's many Mosedales. The area is something of a wilderness—it seems hard to imagine that Longsleddale is not much more than a mile or so away. **Tarn Crag** is reached at **488078** and **2,176ft**, an altogether pleasant place to pause awhile.

193. The next top is Grey Crag (another one) and this can be awkward for no other reason but boggy ground. This part of the day is laborious and the summit is more than usually welcome. **Grey Crag** top is found at **2,093ft (ref. 497072)**; it is the most S.E. point of our tour. If there is time a walk over to Harrop Pike is well worthwhile (you're nearly on the M6 by this time).

194. The 1½ mile drop to Sodgill will prove to be a tiresome business but the ascent of Shipmans Knott should present little difficulty. From the route it is generally N. and N.E. until **Kentmere Pike** is reached at **465077** and **2,397ft**. The top indicates none of its rugged eastern profile which this tour avoided due to timing considerations.

195 & 196. The north-easterly amble over **Brown Howe** at **461083** and **2,300ft** surprisingly gives up the first of these two tops. Froswick on the western horizon appears a huge hill. **Harter Fell** is attained at **460093** and **2,539ft**. From here the outlook is really magnificent, ranking in my opinion with the best in the National Park—Haweswater is stretched out beneath this lofty guardian and added to the associated hills it makes a rewarding scene.

197. Now the day is almost over, but not quite, for **Adam Seat** stands like a sentinel watching over Gatesgarth Pass. This top is reached at **471090** and **2,180ft**. The dregs of the coffee vanished, its down into the pass and back to Mardale Head after a very good round.

13/14 miles; approx. 5,000ft of ascent.

Day 26

Tops 198 - 202 inclusive

Start and finish at Haweswater

198. Kidsty Pike   200.   Rough Crag
199. High Street   201 & 202. Mardale Ill Bell

Schematic/Cartographic Route

(**Warning:** Always consult Ordnance Survey Map, ensure good use
of compass).

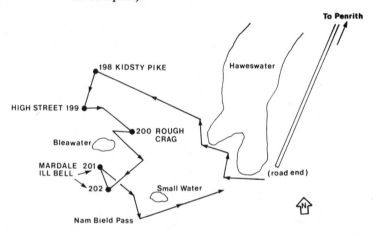

198.   Start and finish at Haweswater. This, the final journey,
is in my eyes a marvellous day to end with. Leaving the
car at Mardale Head, the walker sets off round the western shores
of Haweswater until the mouth of Riggindale is underneath one's
feet. From here the track is followed leading up to **Kidsty Pike**
at **447126** and **2,560ft**. This is a place to come back to time and time
again, an inspiration for the remainder of the day.

199.   Continue west, keeping to the crags, soon brings up the
wall that runs all the way and beyond to the summit
of **High Street**. The valley of Riggindale lies on your left making
this grand tour an enjoyable finale—this historic roadway will have
seen many a weary traveller in days gone by. The cairn is found
on the summit at **441110** and **2,718ft**—here strangely is probably
the least interesting place of the day.

200.   Heading north a little locate the pile of stones that marks the top of Long Stile. This falls in an easterly direction to **Rough Crag,** which is an excellent descent. From the ridge you get a delightful view of Blea Tarn on the right and Haweswater ahead. The top at **454113** and **2,062ft** is a superb resting point before the final section, a time to let the mind wander.

201 & 202. Descend a short distance back towards Long Stile before taking a line down to Blea Tarn. Pause awhile before setting off up again, this time being the best of the day. There are two ways I have taken; either go east of Piot Crag to Small Water joining up with Nan Bield Pass and on to the tops, or follow a steep but more direct way up a rocky spur. The first top for me is the lesser of the two at **448098** and **2,400 + ft;** this is much less significant than the last top at **448101** and **2,496ft** —this is my finish. **Mardale Ill Bell** is a relatively remote point but a grand finishing place. Drop down to Nan Bield Pass and then descend past Small Water to achieve Mardale Head and the car at last.

Not a long day but a good one.

9/10 miles; approx. 3,500ft of ascent.

The Finish and the Future

I DO NOT propose to promise beer to all who complete this challenge, but on a more sober note I would offer my congratulations to those who do complete the tops. This exercise should have been interesting, but to put it into perspective—one must refer again to the Munros of Scotland, mindful of Hamish Brown's magnificent achievement of 'doing' them all in one continuous journey. The Lake District National Park too has its 'hard men' and perhaps that well-known figure, Joss Naylor, should take a high place for it is he who has done so much to popularise challenges and the competitive spirit in the fells.

The next years for me will I hope bring new dimensions, but whatever comes I will use this great 'back garden' as the basis for my walking—for without doubt there is so much still to see and so many things still to do. As the prospect of a difference in the approach to work materialises, this then is my scheme.

The Peaks

Fell Top	Ref.	Height (Ft.)
1. Great Calva	291312	2,265
2. Sale How	277286	2,200 +
3. Lonscale Fell	286271	2,344
4. Little Man	267278	2,837
5. Skiddaw	261291	3,053
6. Carl Side	255281	2,400 +
7. Longside	249284	2,405
8. Carrock Fell	342336	2,174
9. High Pike	319350	2,157
10. Great Lingy Hill	310339	2,000 +
11. Great Lingy Hill	303338	2,000 +
12. Great Sca Fell	292338	2,100 +
13. Great Sca Fell	291342	2,050 +
14. Knott	296330	2,329
15. Coomb Height	311327	2,058
16. Blencathra	323277	2,847
17. Knowe Crags	312270	2,600 +
18. Bannerdale Crags	336290	2,200 +
19. Bannerdale Crags	329296	2,100 +
20. Bowscale Fell	333305	2,306
21. Bowscale Fell	340310	2,200 +
22. Whiteside	171219	2,317
23. Whiteside	174222	2,250 +
24. Hopegill Head	186224	2,525
25. Ladyside Pike	185228	2,300 +
26. Grasmoor	175203	2,791
27. Wandope	188197	2,533
28. Whitelass Pike	180190	2,159
29. Grisedale Pike	199226	2,593
30. Grisedale Pike	193221	2,300 +
31. Eel Crag Hill	193203	2,749
32. Sail	199203	2,500 +
33. Scar Crags	208206	2,205
34. Causey Pike	219209	2,000 +
35. Nitting Haws	236170	2,050 +
36. High Spy	234162	2,143
37. Dalehead	223153	2,473
38. Hindscarth	214160	2,200 +
39. Hindscarth	216165	2,385
40. Robinson	202168	2,417
41. Great Borne	125165	2,000 +
42. Great Borne	124164	2,019
43. Starling Dodd	142157	2,085
44. Red Pike	160154	2,479
45. Dodd	165158	2,050 +
46. Chapel Crags	164150	2,400
47. High Stile	170148	2,644
48. High Crag	180140	2,443
49. Iron Crag	124119	2,100 +
50. Caw Fell	132110	2,288
51. Little Gowder Crag	140110	2,350 +
52. Haycock	145107	2,618
53. Seatallan	140084	2,266
54. Yewbarrow	173085	2,058
55. Stirrup Crag	176093	2,009
56. Red Pike	166106	2,707
57. Scoat Fell	160114	2,760
58. Scoat Fell	158114	2,750 +
59. Scoat Fell	154111	2,750 +
60. Steeple	158116	2,687
61. Black Crag	164116	2,689
62. Pillar	171121	2,927
63. Looking Stead	186118	2,058
64. Kirk Fell	195105	2,630
65. Kirk Fell	199108	2,550 +
66. Slight Side	210050	2,499
67. Cam Spout Crag	209059	2,850
68. Scafell	207063	3,162
69. Scafell Pike	215072	3,210
70. Scafell Pike	221068	2,500 +
71. Scafell Pike	220069	2,500 +

Fell Top	Ref.	Height (Ft.)	Fell Top	Ref.	Height (Ft.)
72. Broad Crag	219076	3,054	119. Walna Scar	258964	2,000 +
73. Ill Crag	223075	3,040	120. Walna Scar	254957	2,000 +
74. Ill Crag	224079	2,950 +	121. Old Man of Coniston	272978	2,635
75. Great End	227084	2,984			
76. Esk Pike	237075	2,903	122. Brim Fell	271986	2,611
77. Lingmell	209082	2,649	123. Swirl How	273005	2,630
78. Seathwaite Fell	227095	2,025 +	124. Wetherlam	283008	2,400 +
			125. Wetherlam	289008	2,400 +
79. Seathwaite Fell	230093	2,000 +	126. Wetherlam	288011	2,502
			127. Ullscarf	292122	2,370
80. Allen Crags	237085	2,572	128. High Raise	281095	2,500
81. Allen Crags	241092	2,200 +	129. Sargeant Man	286089	2,414
82. Allen Crags	243097	2,350 +	130. Seat Sandal	344115	2,415
83. Allen Crags	246102	2,550 +	131. Fairfield	358117	2,863
84. Glaramara	247106	2,560	132. Great Rigg Man	356104	2,513
85. Glaramara	250108	2,300 +	133. Rydal Fell	356095	2,000 +
86. Cam Crag	256114	2,000 +	134. Rydal Fell	356093	2,000 +
87. Base Brown	225114	2,120	135. Rydal Fell	356092	2,022
88. Green Gable	215107	2,603	136. Rydal Fell	356091	2,000 +
89. Great Gable	211103	2,949	137. Erne Crag	357087	2,000 +
90. Brandreth	215119	2,344	138. Heron Pike	355083	2,003
91. Grey Knotts	219126	2,287	139. Clough Head	334225	2,381
92. Fleetwith Pike	213141	2,050 +	140. Calfhow Pike	330211	2,166
93. Fleetwith Pike	211141	2,050 +	141. Randerside	349211	2,250 +
94. Fleetwith Pike	206142	2,126	142. Great Dodd	342204	2,807
95. Tongue Head	241080	2,250 +	143. Stybarrow Dodd	343189	2,750 +
96. Bow Fell	245069	2,825 +	144. Stybarrow Dodd	341186	2,756
97. Bow Fell	245067	2,850 +	145. Sheffield Pike	369182	2,232
98. Bow Fell	245064	2,960	146. Hartside	362195	2,350 +
99. Shelter Crags	249054	2,650 +	147. Hartside	359197	2,481
100. Crinkle Crags	249052	2,680	148. Greenside	353187	2,600 +
101. Crinkle Crags	249051	2,730	149. Raise	343174	2,889
102. Crinkle Crags	249050	2,740	150. Whiteside	338166	2,832
103. Crinkle Crags	248049	2,816	151. Helvellyn	341151	3,118
104. Crinkle Crags	250046	2,733	152. Catstycam	348158	2,917
105. Red How	251034	2,426	153. Birkhouse Moor	365163	2,318
106. Great Knott	260043	2,200 +	154. Birkhouse Moor	363159	2,350 +
107. Cold Pike	264035	2,259(nr)	155. Birkhouse Moor	361158	2,300 +
108. Pike O'Blisco	271042	2,304	156. Birkhouse Moor	360157	2,300 +
109. Thunacar Knott	279081	2,351	157. Striding Edge	351149	2,832
110. Thunacar Knott	279079	2,362	158. Nethermost Pike	344141	2,920
111. Harrison Stickle	282073	2,403	159. High Crag	343136	2,850 +
112. Pike O'Stickle	274074	2,323	160. Dollywagon Pike	346130	2,810
113. Rossett Pike	250075	2,106			
114. Harter Fell	218997	2,140	161. St. Sunday Crag	369134	2,756
115. Great Carrs	270010	2,575	162. Birks	382145	2,040
116. Grey Friar	260004	2,536	163. Hart Crag	369112	2,698
117. Dow Crag	263978	2,555	164. Dove Crag	374104	2,603
118. Brown Pike	261966	2,237	165. Little Hart Crag	384101	2,000 +

Fell Top	Ref.	Height (Ft.)	Fell Top	Ref.	Height (Ft.)
166. Little Hart Crag	387100	2,091	183. Red Crag	450153	2,328
167. Red Screes	396087	2,541	184. Wether Hill	455163	2,210
168. Hartsop Dodd	411118	2,018	185. Wether Hill	456167	2,200 +
169. John Bell's Banner	413100	2,474	186. Loadpot Hill	457181	2,201
			187. Place Fell	405169	2,154
170. Stoney Core Pike	418100	2,502	188. Round How	409166	2,000 +
			189. Selside Pike	491112	2,142
171. Thornthwaite Crag	431100	2,569	190. Branstree	487103	2,200
			191. Branstree	478100	2,333
172. Froswick	435085	2,359	192. Tarn Crag	488078	2,176
173. Ill Bell	436077	2,476	193. Grey Crag	497072	2,093
174. Yoke	438067	2,309	194. Kentmere Pike	465077	2,397
175. Gray Crag	429110	2,331	195. Brown Howe	461083	2,300 +
176. Gray Crag	428114	2,286	196. Harter Fell	460093	2,539
177. Gray Crag	426118	2,250	197. Adam Seat	471090	2,180
178. Rest Dodd	432136	2,278	198. Kidsty Pike	447126	2,560
179. The Knott	437127	2,423	199. High Street	441110	2,718
180. Rampsgill Head	444128	2,581	200. Rough Crag	454113	2,062
181. High Raise	448134	2,634	201. Mardale Ill Bell	448098	2,400 +
182. Raven Howe	450144	2,358	202. Mardale Ill Bell	448101	2,496